Long-Ago Lives

SECRETS OF THE UNEXPLAINED

Long-Ago Lives

by Gary L. Blackwood

BENCHMARK BOOKS

MARSHALL CAVENDISH
NEW YORK

Benchmark Books
Marshall Cavendish Corporation
99 White Plains Road
Tarrytown, New York 10591

Library of Congress Cataloging-in-Publication Data
Blackwood, Gary L.
Long-ago lives / by Gary L. Blackwood.
p.   cm. — (Secrets of the unexplained)
Includes bibliographical references and index.
Summary: Examines reincarnation, discussing past lives, age regression through hypnosis,
spontaneous memory, false memory, karma, and notable case studies.
ISBN 0-7614-0747-2
1. Reincarnation—Juvenile literature. [1. Reincarnation.]
I. Title. II. Series: Blackwood, Gary L. Secrets of the unexplained.
BL515.B53   1999   133.9'01'35—dc21   98-29094   CIP   AC

Photo research by Debbie Needleman
Front cover: Courtesy of Hess/The Image Bank; back cover: Courtesy of Coneyl Jay/Tony Stone Images; page
11: Charles Walker Collection/Stock Montage; page 13: National Portrait Gallery, Smithsonian Institution/Art
Resource, NY; The Image Bank: pages 14–15: Deborah Roundtree; page 31: J-F Podevin; pages 40–41:
Dominic Rouse; page 51: Sandy King; page 53: Philip M. Prosen; page 64: Laurie Rubin; pages 68, 70:
Michel Tcherevkoff; page 18: Ellen Martorelli/ Tony Stone Images; page 20: Oscar Burriel, Latin Stock/Science
Photo Library/ Photo Researchers; page 21: Alison Wright/ Photo Researchers: page 24: Metro-Goldwyn Mayer
(Courtesy of Kobal); page 28: David Parker/Science Photo Library/Photo Researchers; page 33: / Reuters/Jason
Bye/Archive Photos; page 36: Erich Lessing/Art Resource, NY; page 44: Orin A. Sealy/Denver Post; page 45:
Paramount (Courtesy of Kobal); page 47: Denver Post; page 57 (both): Dr. Elmar R.Gruber /Fortean Picture
Library; page 59: Ian Cook/ People Weekly, c.1994;   page 60: Mary Evans Picture Library.

Printed in Hong Kong

1   3   5   6   4   2

*To the helpful staff at the Carthage Public Library
who cheerfully put up with my sometimes strange requests.*

Contents

Introduction

Has this ever happened to you?

• You enter a town or building that you know you've never visited before. But for some reason, the place seems very familiar. You have a sense of knowing what lies around the next corner, even what's going to happen next. It's as if you're watching a movie you thought was new, and then you realize you've seen it before. In fact, the term for this phenomenon, déjà vu, means "seen before."

• A preschool brother or sister, cousin, niece or nephew tells you matter-of-factly about what it was like "when I used to be big."

• You have an especially vivid and detailed dream set in some other time or place, a setting you don't remember ever reading about.

• You're introduced to someone for the first time, and find yourself with an instant and intense liking—or disliking—for the person. You have the feeling you've met before, maybe even known each other for a long, long time.

Well, maybe you have. And it could be that you've been in that "new" town or building before, and that you've actually experienced the events from that vivid dream. That young child may once have been "big," too. If the theory of reincarnation is right, all these things may have come to pass in a previous life.

A *previous* life? We all joke about cats having nine lives. Myths tell about the phoenix, a great bird that dies in a burst of flame, then rises from its own ashes. And there are dozens of legends of heroes like King Arthur, who promise to come back to life when the world needs them. But how many people seriously believe that animals and people have lived before and will come back again after this life is over?

A lot, actually. According to Dr. Raymond A. Moody Jr., psychiatrist and best-selling author, it's "possibly the oldest and most widely held spiritual belief known to mankind." The concept has had a number of names: metempsychosis, palingenesis, preexistence, or simply rebirth. In the middle of the nineteenth century, the term *reincarnation* came into use, and it has stuck around ever since.

Most people who haven't studied reincarnation much think it's strictly the property of Eastern religions such as Hinduism and Buddhism. And certainly it's easier to find someone who believes in past lives if you look in a Buddhist or Hindu country such as India. In fact, there it may be hard to find someone who *doesn't* believe in past lives.

But Asians have no monopoly on the idea. It's been a crucial part of nearly every culture and religion, in nearly every part of the world, since the Stone Age. It's turned up in Ireland and Iceland; in Africa and Australia; in Prussia, Persia, and Polynesia; in Greece and Germany; in Turkey and Tibet; in Bali, Burma, and Brazil—and, yes, in North America, too. When Europeans invaded the New World,

According to the Hindu sacred poem The Bhagavad Gita, *"As a man leaves an old garment and puts on one that is new, the Spirit leaves his mortal body and then puts on one that is new."*

some Native American tribes didn't resist because they believed the white men were the reincarnation of an older race of people who once ruled the land and had come to reclaim it.

A strong belief in reincarnation had quite the opposite effect on the Celtic peoples of Ireland in the first and second centuries B.C. They were such fierce and fearless fighters that the Romans couldn't conquer Ireland, as they had England. Julius Caesar speculated that the Celts were so brave because they didn't fear death. They were certain that, when they died, their souls would pass into a new body.

In many cultures, when a child is born, its parents look for some sign—a distinctive birthmark, for example—that the baby is the rein-carnation of a family member who has died. If the Vikings found such evidence, they named the child after the dead relative. The Yoruba of West Africa often named a baby boy Babatunde, meaning "Father has returned," and a baby girl Yetunde—"Mother has returned."

Some of the best and brightest minds in history have bought the concept of past lives. One of the first reincarnationists on record is Pythagoras, the sixth-century B.C. Greek mathematician. He was sure that, in a past life, he'd been wounded during the siege of Troy. He once stopped a man from beating a dog because he recognized, in the dog's yelps, the voice of a dead friend.

Benjamin Franklin wrote, "I believe I shall, in some shape or other, always exist." Louisa May Alcott has achieved immortality through her books, but she believed in a more literal sort of immor-tality: "I think immortality is the passing of a soul through many lives or experiences."

Those practical-minded American inventors Henry Ford and Thomas Edison were both convinced that we go around more than once. Ford wrote that "souls come and go, and they come again, prepared by past experience for greater achievement." He felt that his mechanical genius, like Mozart's musical genius, must have been carried over from a previous life. Presumably it wasn't Ford's most recent one. In that existence, he thought, he'd been a Civil War soldier who met his end at the Battle of Gettysburg. That could explain why Ford was such an outspoken pacifist.

Early in his life, Ford was puzzled by such questions as "Where do we come from?" and "What happens to us after we die?" and

"Why do some people have an easy life, and others suffer?" Reincarnation seemed to offer the best explanation. It made him feel better, too, to think that all the work he'd put in as he struggled for success wouldn't be wasted, that it would benefit him in his next life. "Work is futile," he wrote, "if we cannot utilise the experience we collect in one life in the next."

Thomas Edison's view of reincarnation was less philosophical than Ford's. He tried to explain the process in scientific terms: "The unit of life is composed of swarms of billions of highly charged entities which live in the cells. I believe that when a man dies, this swarm deserts the body . . . and enters another cycle of life and is immortal."

Thomas Edison speculated that the human personality survives after death. He hoped to build a scientific device that would amplify messages from the spirit world.

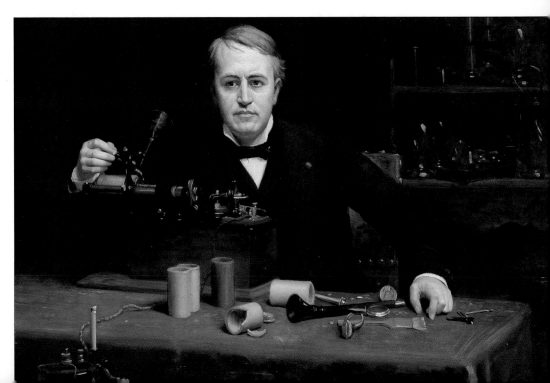

PART ONE

The
Theories

How It Works

In Edison's day, or in Ben Franklin's, it took quite a bit of courage to talk about more than one life, at least in a country where most people were Christians. Though very early Christians did accept reincarnation, in A.D. 553, the Second Council of Constantinople outlawed the belief. Apparently the church feared that, if people were counting on a future life, they'd do whatever they wanted to in this one.

Actually, according to most philosophies, reincarnation doesn't encourage irresponsible behavior at all. In fact, it promotes and rewards moral behavior, through a concept called karma.

Karma is philosophy's version of the computer maxim "Garbage in, garbage out," or the much older saying "You reap what you sow." In other words, what you dish out in this life determines what you get back in the next one. Let's say, for example, that you're a bully who picks on the weak and helpless. In your next life, you might be the weak and helpless one, so you can learn how it feels.

Some cultures believe that karma can be even harsher. If you lead a really rotten life, they say, you're liable to come back as an animal, an insect, a vegetable, even an inanimate object. This concept is called transmigration. It provides parents in those cultures with a tool for disciplining their kids that carries more weight than the promise of a spanking or a grounding: "If you don't behave, you'll be a cockroach in your next life!"

Most serious students of reincarnation, though, don't think it's likely that a person could come back as a cow or a turnip. They say that, though we may start out on the bottom rung of the evolutionary

Praying with a Purr

When a cat began turning up regularly at a temple in Kuala Lumpur, worshippers suspected the animal might be the reincarnation of some fellow Buddhist. What made them think so? During prayers, the cat often sat up on its haunches with its paws in the air, as if it were praying, too.

ladder, once we earn enough good karma to work our way up to the level of a human, we never slip back to a lower level.

The way most reincarnationists explain it, the whole process of rebirth and karma works much the way public school does. Each lifetime is like a new grade, in which we learn lessons that make us wiser and more compassionate. If you don't learn what you need to, you may have to repeat the grade, sometimes over and over until you get it right. Then you move onward and upward.

Between the grades, or lifetimes, is a sort of summer vacation called the interregnum or Bardo state. In this disembodied state, the spirit rests and thinks about the lessons it's learned—or failed to learn—and how to apply that knowledge to the next life. Then it chooses a life that will reinforce those lessons, and will help make up for the mistakes made in the previous life. A group of souls may even choose to be reborn in the same time and place, in order to work out troubled past relationships.

When a mother learned at a past-life seminar about this concept of choosing your next life, she turned to her daughter and said, "See, you chose me, so stop blaming me!" The daughter fired back, "Then I must have been in a hurry."

If we can mull things over in that disembodied state, why do we have to learn our lessons the hard way? Why do we go to all the trouble of living one life after another in the physical world, with all its problems and pain? Why not just kick back in the Bardo state and watch others make the mistakes, and learn from that? Because, the theory goes, in order to *really* understand something, you have to experience it firsthand.

Some reincarnationists teach that physical life is meant to be only a temporary state. When the spirit leaves the body, they say, it is returning to its normal plane of existence.

Apparently each spirit decides how long a vacation it needs after a given experience. Those who have had a particularly grueling life may decide to sit on the sidelines for a while, considering what to do next. Others jump right back into the physical world. According to psychic Edgar Cayce, these eager beavers tend to fall into one of three categories: 1) Those who made a big mistake late in life and want to correct it quickly, 2) Those whose lives were cut short before they accomplished what they wanted to, and 3) Those who want to come back in order to help others cope with their lives.

Tibetan Buddhists believe that, when their high priest or Dalai Lama dies, his spirit comes back almost immediately, as a newborn

The child who is destined to be the next Dalai Lama may suspect it before anyone else does. "Even before I was recognized," writes the current Dalai Lama, "I often told my mother that I was going to go to Lhasa [Tibet's capital]. I used to straddle a window sill in our house pretending that I was riding a horse to Lhasa."

baby. About two years after a Dalai Lama's death, the other priests, following leads given by psychics and predictions made by the Dalai Lama himself, start a full-scale search for a child who shows signs of being their reincarnated master. When they find a likely prospect, they put him to the test by setting an array of objects before him to see if he can pick out the ones that belonged to the late Dalai Lama.

Many Happy Returns

 In our part of the world, after centuries of being frowned upon by the church, reincarnation is experiencing a rebirth. A 1996 Gallup poll revealed that 22 percent of American adults believe in past and future lives. In experiments at Chicago State University, researchers hypnotized volunteers and tried to dig up some knowledge of a past life. In ninety-three out of one hundred cases, they succeeded.

Movie stars the likes of Glenn Ford, Shirley MacLaine, and Sylvester Stallone have talked freely about their former lives. Stallone feels that, in one life, he was a wolf; in another he was beheaded during the French Revolution.

Reincarnation has even become part of our popular culture. Hollywood has explored the possibilities in such movies as *Fluke*, *Heaven Can Wait*, and *Groundhog Day*. A greeting card featuring cartoon character Ziggy reads:

Enjoy yourself on your birthday. Remember, you only live once. But, just in case you believe in reincarnation, MANY HAPPY RETURNS!

Transmigration, the idea that a person may be reborn as an animal, has largely fallen out of favor—except in Hollywood. In the 1994 film Fluke, a man killed in a car crash comes back as a dog.

The concept of reincarnation is an appealing one. If it's true, it means that we don't get just one chance at life. It also means we don't just have to regret our mistakes; we can make up for them.

But for most of us, the fact that an idea is appealing isn't reason enough to accept it. We need convincing evidence, not just theories. If we really have lived before, why can't we remember those lives? That would be pretty convincing.

It would also be pretty amazing, considering that most of us remember only a fraction of the things that have happened to us in *this* life. It's probably just as well. If we could remember everything we've ever learned or experienced, it would be overwhelming. Imagine how much more mind-boggling it would be, then, to remember in full a bunch of past lives.

As Mohandas Gandhi put it, "It is nature's kindness that we do not remember past births. . . . Life would be a burden if we carried such a tremendous load of memories." The ancient Greeks believed that, when they were born again, they drank from the river Lethe, whose water made them forget their past lives.

The fact that a person has no conscious memory of something doesn't mean that it's not stored somewhere in the mind. With the right stimulation, our brains can call up things we'd forgotten we ever knew.

Sometimes it happens by accident. For example, an unusual smell can trigger a vivid image of a time when we smelled the same scent before. And sometimes we can access those buried memories deliberately, through some technique such as meditation or hypnosis.

If our brains hold memories of past lives, too, then doesn't it stand to reason that we should be able to tap into those memories in the same ways? Some people believe that we can and that, either accidentally or deliberately, thousands of us have done so.

Past-Life Therapy

The most successful method of dredging up memories of previous lives is called past-life regression. Sometimes it's used deliberately; other times it happens by accident, as part of a technique called age regression. Psychologists and psychiatrists have been using age regression for years, as a way of quickly getting to the root of their patients' deep-seated emotional problems.

Using hypnosis, age regression therapists take the patient back through his or her own life, sometimes all the way to the moment of birth, even to life in the mother's womb. Logically, that seems to be the end of the road, as far back as a patient can regress. But a few therapists have pressed on, and asked the patient to go further back, to a time before the problem began. And sometimes an astounding thing happens: the patient begins describing another life, very different from the current one.

Surprisingly, past-life regression isn't a new technique. In fact, it dates back almost as far as the use of hypnosis. In 1862, under hypnosis, an uneducated German woman began speaking in fluent

French about a life she'd led in Brittany a hundred years earlier, in which she threw her husband off a cliff. When her hypnotist traveled to Brittany, he found that the woman described by his subject had really existed.

Between 1893 and 1904, Colonel Albert de Rochas, a Frenchman, regressed nineteen subjects during what he called "magnetic sleep." One of them, a nineteen-year-old girl named Josephine, revealed a whole series of past lives—as a wicked old woman, a baby, a ruthless bandit, and an ape. De Rochas even claimed to have taken Josephine forward in time as far as 1970, and gotten details of two *future* lives!

In 1906, Dr. Morris Stark, a New York physician, recorded in shorthand several sessions with a young woman who recalled in accurate detail her lives in ancient Rome and Egypt.

In recent years, psychologists and psychiatrists have been using past-life regression deliberately as a type of therapy, with amazing success. Not only does it help cure emotional problems such as fears and depression, it can also help with physical illnesses such as asthma, ulcers, and arthritis.

How can experiencing a past life possibly help us deal with problems in our present life? Let's look at some actual case histories.

Joe, a man in his midthirties, had a bad case of insomnia. He just didn't seem to be able to relax enough to sleep soundly. When he was

Psychologists have found that 90 percent of patients who are asked under hypnosis to recall a past life will do so.

hypnotized and regressed, he recalled a former life as a marshal in a Colorado frontier town. For years, he'd had to stay constantly on the alert and could sleep only in quick catnaps. After Joe experienced this past life, he was able to really relax for the first time, and his insomnia vanished.

A woman plagued by painful migraine headaches also uncovered a previous life in the Old West. She'd been a saloon girl who died of a gunshot wound to the head—right in the spot where her headaches always started. After the therapy, the headaches stopped.

A teenage swimmer found herself suddenly terrified at the prospect of diving into the swimming pool. Under hypnosis, she became a Louisiana girl who, just before she jumped into a swimming hole, saw a shadowy shape beneath the surface of the water. The shape turned out to be a hungry alligator. Once she understood the reason behind her fear, the girl conquered it and went on to win many diving medals.

Novelist Taylor Caldwell had a lifelong fascination with the nine-teenth-century author George Eliot. In fact, when Caldwell was only six, she recounted the whole plot of Eliot's *The Mill on the Floss*, even though she'd never read the book or had it read to her.

Caldwell was sure she couldn't be hypnotized. Nevertheless she was regressed hypnotically, and described life as a twelve-year-old scullery maid in George Eliot's household. When the girl was slow or disobedient, the housekeeper boxed her ears, sometimes so severely that they bled. Caldwell had long had trouble with increasing deafness. When she came out of her trance, her hearing had improved dramatically.

In many cases past-life regression under hypnosis can get to the root of a physical or emotional problem far more quickly than traditional therapy.

Though the hypnotist uncovered several more of her past lives, Caldwell scorned the notion of reincarnation. "I shudder," she said, "at the very thought of being born again into this world."

Past-life regression can work on a subject as skeptical as Caldwell, but it's a lot easier if the subject is open to the idea. In 1983 a psychologist at the University of Kentucky hypnotized three groups and regressed them, but only after playing a tape for them. The first group's tape enthusiastically promoted past-life therapy. The second group's tape said that it might or might not work. The third group's tape made past-life regression sound far-out and flaky. Of the students from group one, 83 percent went on to recall at least one past life. Sixty percent of group two did so, but only 10 percent of group three. Obviously one of the keys to successfully calling up a past life is to believe you can.

In fact, other research indicates that nearly anyone who's receptive to the idea can recall past lives under hypnosis. That doesn't mean that everyone *should*. It can be an unnerving experience. Subjects often reveal lives of misery and oppression that end in violent deaths. What's more, they recall them so vividly that it's like living through them.

At best, past lives tend to be so totally ordinary that the subject

Though most subjects of past-life regression recall a perfectly ordinary, even drab, existence, a few lay claim to a distinguished past. This London man, who believes he is the reincarnation of the legendary King Arthur, was once arrested for carrying a deadly weapon—a sword he calls Excalibur.

is disappointed. Very rarely does anyone remember being a famous historical personage. Even when someone does recall a notable past life, the famous person the subject identifies with is not necessarily someone admirable. A Missouri college student recalled a former life as President Lincoln's assassin (see Part Two, "Possible Proofs"). A medical doctor discovered he'd once been John Dillinger, the Chicago criminal who was declared "public enemy number one" in the 1930s.

Because past-life regression can call up unpleasant, even traumatic experiences, most therapists are careful how and when they use it.

True or False?

 Though there's no denying that past-life regression is a valuable tool, not all therapists who use it are convinced that what they're dealing with are former lives in the literal sense. Scientists and scholars have offered a number of other possible explanations.

Since most regressions take the form of a question-and-answer session, with the hypnotist asking the questions, some speculate that subjects are just following the hypnotist's lead, saying what they think the hypnotist wants to hear. And it's true that subjects under hypnosis are very suggestible and anxious to please.

A second theory says that, since psychic powers often increase under hypnosis, the subject may in effect be reading the hypnotist's mind. The flaw in both these theories is that often the subject comes up with detailed information about a time and place the hypnotist has no knowledge of.

According to a third theory, the subject is doing just what we all do when we're dreaming: digging up bits and pieces of information from the unconscious mind and stringing them together in a sort of fantasy story.

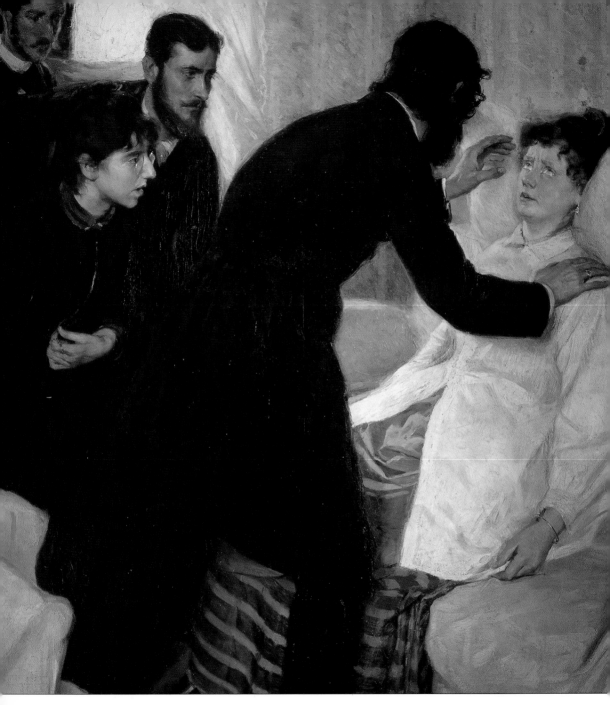

The use of hypnosis as a therapeutic tool dates back to the beginning of the nineteenth century.

On the face of it, this seems to be the most logical and likely hypothesis. But it doesn't explain how some subjects can know facts about a time period or country they've never even read about. Occasionally, subjects even start speaking in a language that's totally unfamiliar to them. This strange ability is called xenoglossy. One example is the man who recalled a past life as a Viking in A.D. 1000. He demonstrated a good command of ancient Norse, the language a Viking would have spoken. Another subject, who described a life in early Mesopotamia, could write sentences in Sassanid Pahlavi, a language that hasn't been used since A.D. 651. Yet another man, who had been an Egyptian priest in 2000 B.C., could speak ancient Egyptian and write hieroglyphics.

In an attempt to account for this kind of obscure knowledge, some scholars point to a phenomenon known as cryptomnesia—the mind's ability to remember information that was once learned, then forgotten. And there are some amazing cases in which cryptomnesia was obviously at work.

One involves a doctor who "became" Mark Twain very convincingly under hypnosis. The subject insisted that he knew nothing about the humorist's life or work. But when the therapist dug deeper, his subject revealed that he had been forced to read quite a lot of Twain's writing in high school, and had resented it so much that his conscious mind had blocked out the experience.

It is hard to imagine, though, putting out the time and effort required to learn a whole different language, especially a long-dead one, and then not being able to remember that you'd done so.

In any case, the above theories are just that—theories. There's been little effort made to prove them. The theory of reincarnation, on the other hand, is supported by some pretty solid evidence, gathered by respected researchers such as Dr. Helen Wambach.

Over a period of several years, Dr. Wambach hypnotically regressed 750 subjects, in groups of 10 to 12. After each session, the subjects answered a long list of questions about daily life and customs in the country and time period they'd "visited." Dr. Wambach had historians check the answers. The details provided by the subjects about such matters as religion, dress, food, and money were astonishingly accurate. Her subjects were just as convincing in the things they omitted as in the things they included. They didn't talk much about the big historical events that most of us would associate with a certain time or place. Instead, they recounted the humdrum lives of ordinary people.

As a result of her research, Wambach says, "I don't believe in reincarnation—I know it." If a thousand people tell you "they have crossed a bridge in Pennsylvania, you are convinced of the existence of that bridge in Pennsylvania."

Yet no amount of secondhand testimony actually *proves* that the bridge exists. And as impressive as Wambach's findings are, they don't prove beyond a reasonable doubt that her subjects have lived before. Theoretically, they could have come across the information in a book.

Just what *does* constitute proof, then? What would convince you? How about if a subject recalled specific details that can't be found in a history book, then you checked on them and found that those details were accurate?

That's called external verification, and it's pretty rare. Most past-life therapists don't have the time, the money, or the inclination to check up on what their subjects have told them. But a few have taken that extra step, and have turned up some pretty convincing external verification.

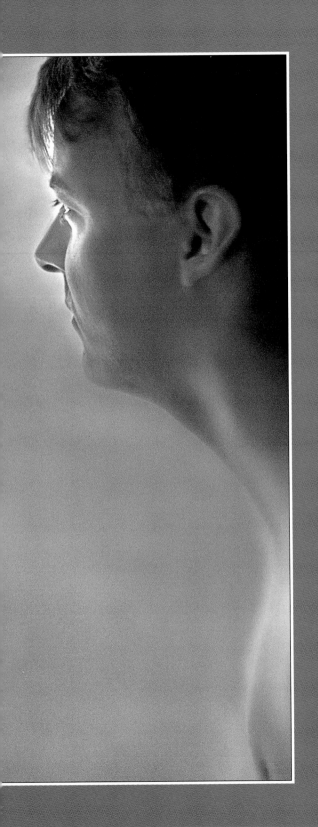

PART TWO

The
Evidence

Possible Proofs

 Probably the most famous and most controversial account of past-life regression appeared in 1956, in the best-selling book *The Search for Bridey Murphy*. It was written by a Colorado businessman named Morey Bernstein, who was also an experienced hypnotist.

Bernstein had always scoffed at the idea of reincarnation, but after reading about the "past-life readings" done by psychic Edgar Cayce, he became intrigued, and wondered if he could call up past lives through hypnosis.

In November 1952, he found a willing subject in a twenty-nine-year-old housewife named Virginia Tighe (to protect her privacy, Bernstein calls her Ruth Simmons in the book). The technique of past-life regression wasn't well known or widely used at the time, so Bernstein just winged it. After taking Virginia back through her present life, year by year, he asked her to move back even further, to "some other place, in some other time."

Virginia began to speak in the voice of a four-year-old girl. When Bernstein advanced her to the age of eight, she identified herself as

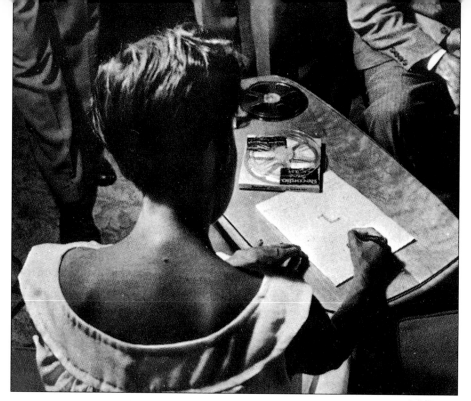

Under hypnosis Virginia Tighe drew a map showing where she lived in her incarnation as Bridey Murphy.

Bridget Kathleen Murphy, nicknamed Bridey. She lived, she said, in Cork, Ireland, in the year 1806. Bridey spoke in a slight Irish accent that grew more pronounced as the sessions went on. Sometimes she used odd, unfamiliar expressions such as "brate," "tup," and "mother socks." A definite personality emerged, too. Unlike Virginia, Bridey was sassy, irreverent, and often impatient.

Bernstein captured the sessions on a tape recorder. Over a period of about a year, Bridey revealed many facts, not only about her childhood but about her adult life, her marriage to Brian MacCarthy, and her death in 1864, at the age of sixty-six. She also described in detail the area of Ireland where she lived. She even recited some of her favorite stories, sang songs of the period, and skillfully performed an Irish jig.

Wanting to share his findings, Bernstein approached New York publishers with his notes, and signed a contract for a book on Bridey. The publisher was so anxious to get the book in print that researchers didn't have time to make a thorough check on the accuracy of Bridey's statements.

When *The Search for Bridey Murphy* was published in 1956, it caused a sensation. Reincarnation was suddenly a hot topic. In many

The movie version of the Bridey Murphy story proved much less interesting than the real thing.

cities, it became a popular pastime to throw "Come As You Were" parties. It seemed as if half the country was eager to explore past lives, and the other half was bent on proving that poor Bridey was a fake.

A series of newspaper articles in the *Chicago American* did the most damage. They claimed, among other things, that 1) Virginia Tighe had grown up with an Irish aunt who told her tales of Ireland, 2) one of her neighbors had been an Irishwoman named Bridie Murphy Corkell, and 3) Virginia had learned in school to dance an Irish jig and to do monologues in an Irish accent.

Life magazine repeated these accusations, and it became widely accepted that Bernstein had been the victim—or perhaps the perpetrator—of a hoax.

But the fact was, only one of the *Chicago American*'s claims was true. Virginia *had* lived near a Mrs. Bridie Corkell, but had never visited her, and didn't even know her first name. Besides, Bridie Corkell came from a different part of Ireland than Bridey Murphy. The evidence against Virginia Tighe seemed even more trumped-up when Mrs. Corkell proved to be the mother of an editor at the *Chicago American*!

The approach taken by the *Denver Post* was much more responsible. That newspaper sent a reporter, William J. Barker, to Ireland for three weeks to investigate Bridey's claims. Official records of births, deaths, and marriages were rare before 1864, so Barker found no trace of Bridey herself. But he did find that "Bridey was dead right on at least two dozen facts Ruth [Virginia's fictional name] simply could not have acquired in this country [the United States]."

Barker verified that the stores where Bridey had bought food

Reporter William J. Barker verified many of the details provided by Bridey Murphy, but couldn't manage to locate the site of Bridey's grave.

actually existed. So did the odd terms she'd used, and the small towns she'd named, which weren't shown on any map. Probably the most convincing elements of Bridey's story, though, were the dates she gave of various events in her life. None were incorrect, and none contradicted each other. Pretty amazing, considering that the sessions took place over a long period of time and that, in each session, Bridey jumped around to different times in her life.

Though Bridey Murphy's case is probably the best-known example of external verification, it's far from the only one. Ten years after Bernstein's encounter with Bridey, a Kansas City hypnotist, Dr. Dell Leonardi, regressed a college student she calls Wesley. The doctor was stunned to find herself in a dialogue with the actor John Wilkes Booth—the man who shot President Lincoln a hundred years earlier.

As in Bridey's case, Booth had a distinct personality very different from Wesley's. Booth was charming, witty, and sarcastic. His voice was that of a trained actor, and his speech was formal, with no trace of 1960s slang.

At first, Booth was sullen and mistrustful, but eventually he warmed to Dr. Leonardi. Even so, it took a year of sessions before Booth would talk about the assassination itself. When he did, he revealed the most startling detail of all: Booth hadn't been killed in a barn in Virginia, as history books said. The man who died there was a decoy. Booth himself escaped to San Francisco, then to London, where he acted in plays under an assumed name. He lived out his last years in Calais, France.

In 1971, Wesley traveled to Europe with Dr. Leonardi. Though it was his first time there, he seemed totally familiar with the streets of London and with a theater where Booth said he had acted. When they crossed on a ferry to France and Wesley caught sight of Calais, his first thought was, "God, I'm coming home!"

Dr. Paul Hansen, a past-life therapist himself, was regressed to a comfortable life as a French nobleman, Antoine Poirot. As Poirot, he'd owned a huge estate outside Vichy, France, in the 1600s. When Hansen researched church records from that place and time period, he found a record of Poirot's birth.

During age regression therapy, an artist named Karl saw himself as a Spanish priest in the midst of a bloody battle outside a stone fortress. He produced a series of sketches of the surroundings, including a drawing of the ring that the priest wore on his finger; the ring had initials carved in it.

On an impulse, Karl spent his next vacation in Ireland, where he came upon the ruins of an old stone fort that seemed familiar. When he researched its history, he learned that in 1580, during one of the Irish revolts against the British, the fort had been taken by English troops under the command of Sir Walter Raleigh. Assisting the Irish were Spanish and Italian soldiers. Raleigh had all six hundred defenders of the fort put to death—including a Spanish priest whose initials were identical to those Karl had seen on his ring.

Out of the Mouths of Babes

There's been a lot of concern in recent years about the phenomenon of "false memory"—subjects recalling under hypnosis things that never really happened to them. Most of the questionable cases involve subjects who "remember" being abused as children, or who reveal under hypnosis that they were kidnapped by aliens.

The fact that we can invent such real-seeming false memories casts doubt on the whole process of using hypnosis to evoke memories—including memories of past lives.

Dr. Ian Stevenson, a psychiatrist who was long considered the leading expert in reincarnation research, felt that most "past lives" brought out by hypnotic regression aren't genuine. Instead, they may be a mixture of "the subject's current personality, his expectations of what he thinks the hypnotist wants, his fantasies of what he thinks his previous life ought to have been, and also perhaps elements derived paranormally." In Stevenson's opinion, the only past-life memories worth studying are the ones that surface on their own from our unconscious minds.

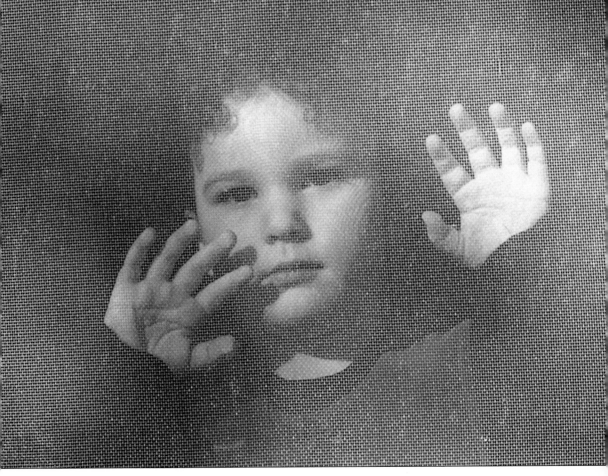

Using young children as the subjects of reincarnation research can be tricky. Because their vocabulary is limited, they may have trouble describing objects and events from a remembered life.

The most valuable of all, he said, come from children under the age of six, "because they do not usually interpret their cases; they just say: 'This is it; my name is so and so.' To them it is very clear, very vivid."

These cases are also the easiest to verify. Hypnosis often calls up lives from the distant past. When kids spontaneously recall a past life, it's nearly always from the very recent past. That means that most of the people who shared that life are still alive, and the places where it was lived are more or less unchanged.

Naturally, a lot of these cases turn up in Asian countries, where reincarnation is accepted as a fact by most people. But even in those countries, *recalling* a past life is often frowned upon, for several reasons.

Buddhists believe that only Buddhas should be able to remember past lives. Hindus fear that a child who talks about a past life will die young. The parents may try to banish those memories by whirling the child around on a potter's wheel, or keep them from being spoken by filling the child's mouth with soap.

Even so, hundreds of cases came to Stevenson's attention, and he investigated many of them in depth. Stevenson wrote, "The case usually starts when a small child of two to four years begins talking to his parents or siblings of a life he led in another time and place. The child usually feels a considerable pull back toward the events of that life and he frequently importunes [begs] his parents to let him return to the community where he claims that he formerly lived."

A boy from Lebanon, Imad Elawar, was a textbook case. When Stevenson met Imad in 1964, the boy was only five, but for several years he had been claiming that he'd lived before, in a village on the other side of the mountain. He described over a dozen people he had known, things he'd owned, such as a shotgun and a small yellow car, and events from his former life.

Stevenson often had to get his evidence secondhand, from witnesses. What made this case so convincing was that, when Imad made his first visit to the site of his previous life, Stevenson came along. They found that the details Imad had given pointed toward a

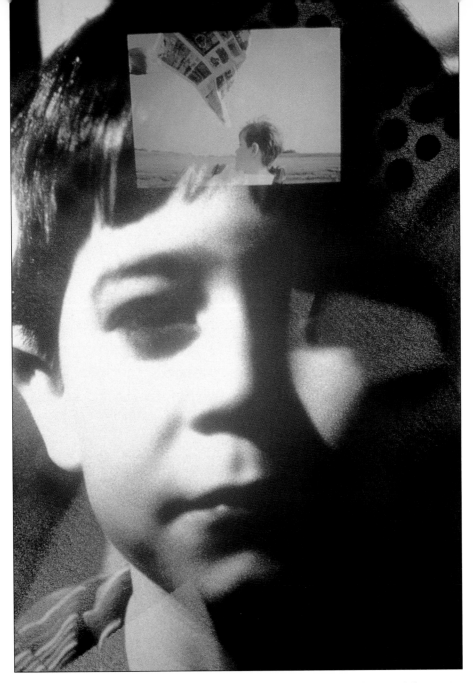

Reincarnation researcher Ian Stevenson found that children with past-life memories often bore a close physical resemblance to the person they claimed to have been.

man named Ibrahim Bouhamzy, who had died of tuberculosis nine years before Imad was born.

They toured Ibrahim's house and met several family members. Imad didn't recognize his "mother," who had aged a lot, but knew his "sister" at once. The family tried to trick him by showing him a photo of Ibrahim and asking whether it was his brother or his uncle. Neither, said Imad; "It was me."

He knew what Ibrahim's dying words had been, and the location of the secret compartment where he had stored his shotgun, and he recalled obscure incidents such as the time his "mother" shut her finger in the door. Stevenson had listed fifty-seven claims made by Imad *before* he met Ibrahim's family. Fifty-one of them proved correct.

In India, Stevenson investigated several cases that closely paralleled Imad's. In all of them, children began describing a previous life when they were between two and four years old.

Of all the countries in North and South America, Brazil is the most accepting of reincarnation, and Stevenson found similar cases there. One of the most intriguing involved a girl named Sinhá, who predicted her own rebirth.

Sinhá died of tuberculosis at the age of twenty-eight. As she lay dying, she told her friend Ida, the wife of the local schoolteacher, that she would come back as Ida's daughter. Ida would recognize her, she said, because the daughter would know details of her life as Sinhá.

Ten months after Sinhá's death, Ida gave birth to a baby girl and named her Marta. When Marta was two and a half, she began telling her family about "when I was Sinhá." Ida had never mentioned

Sinhá's prediction. When she pressed Marta for details about her former life, the girl's replies were uncannily accurate. She knew what Sinhá's last words to Ida had been, and even revealed things about Sinhá's life that Ida hadn't known, but that proved correct.

As she grew older, Marta resembled Sinhá more and more, in her looks and personality, in her love of cats and of dancing, even in her handwriting.

In countries where reincarnation is less accepted, children also talk about "when I was big." It's just that it's more likely to be regarded as a fantasy than as evidence of a past life. Still, compelling cases do crop up here, too, in such seemingly unlikely places as Iowa.

The story of four-year-old Romy Crees is an especially interesting one because, in her previous life, she'd been a man. Her name, she said, had been Joe Williams. She'd lived in Charles City, Iowa, a town 140 miles from Romy's home. She'd been married to a woman named Sheila and had three children. As Joe, she'd died in a motorcycle accident.

Though Romy's family was skeptical, they took her to visit Joe Williams's mother, who still lived in Charles City. Mrs. Williams became friends with Romy at once. She confirmed most of the things Romy had said about Joe's life, and about his death in a motorcycle accident two years before Romy was born.

Spontaneous Memory in Adults

 Children who recall past lives nearly always lose all memory of them as they grow older and go off to school, and develop new interests and friends. But a few people have gone on experiencing those spontaneous memories or had them for the first time as adults with children of their own.

An Ohio steel mill worker named Jack McCord had always been obsessed with airplanes. During World War II, he tried to enlist as a pilot, but his eyesight was too poor. One night he had a realistic dream in which he saw himself as a World War I fighter pilot. Intrigued, McCord tried various methods of tapping his unconscious mind—a Ouija board, automatic writing, consulting psychics. All three methods told him the same thing: in a previous life, he'd been Albert Ball, a British pilot who shot down forty-three German planes and was shot down himself at the age of twenty-one.

McCord did some serious research and found that Albert Ball was a real person who lived and died just as the dreams and the psychic information had said.

Ever since the age of three, Jenny Cockell, an English podiatrist,

Occasionally information about past lives surfaces through the technique of automatic writing, in which the subject's hand seems to write words without conscious guidance. It's not a method to be used casually—the message can be unpredictable, even disturbing.

This example, written in Italian, shows a striking difference between the subject's normal handwriting (below) and that produced by automatic writing (above).

had experienced vivid dreams about a past life in Ireland. In that life, she was Mary Sutton, who died of a fever in 1932, leaving behind eight young children.

When Cockell married and had children of her own, the thought of Mary's orphaned children tormented her. Realizing that some of those children might still be alive, she set about finding them.

First she studied a map of Ireland. She felt drawn to the tiny town of Malahide. When she checked church records, she found that Mary Sutton had indeed lived and died there. Mary's children had been sent to orphanages, or to live with other family members. Cockell tracked them down and brought them all together for the first time in nearly sixty years.

Naturally, they were skeptical of Cockell's claim. But when she recalled for them the smallest details of their mother's life, they couldn't help believing. Mary Sutton's daughter Phyllis marveled that Cockell "knew the pictures on the wall, what was in the house, how it was built. The only thing I can think is that Mammy passed her soul on to this unborn person."

Occasionally, past-life memories are triggered by some physical event in this life. When she was three, Dorothy Eady fell down a flight of stairs at her home in Plymouth, England. At first, her family was certain she was dead. But then Dorothy sat up, crying, and said, "I want to go home." Though they assured her that she was home, she wouldn't be comforted.

From then on, Dorothy was convinced that she belonged in some other place and time. She learned exactly where and when by looking at a photograph of an ancient Egyptian temple. "Here is my

Jenny Cockell (center, right) has the unusual distinction of being younger than her children. She feels that Christy, Phyllis, Betty, Sonny, and Frank were part of her family in a previous incarnation.

home," she said, "but why is it in ruins, and where are the gardens?"

When Dorothy grew up, she got a job with the Egyptian Antiquities Service, helping to excavate and restore the very temple she had recognized as "home." She knew instinctively the exact layout of the temple, and easily translated hieroglyphics that were difficult to decipher.

Had she really lived there, long before? Was Romy Crees once a motorcycle-riding man? Was Wesley actually Lincoln's assassin in a previous life, or was he making it all up?

Probably no one will ever know for sure. But then there are a lot of things in the universe that we can't be sure of. All we can do is look at the evidence and decide whether or not it convinces us.

The most compelling evidence, of course, is personal experience.

Many reincarnation scholars feel that souls tend to be reborn not singly but in groups, so that people who were close in one life will come together again in a later one. In this painting a pair of ancient Egyptian lovers see themselves born again in the twentieth century.

That doesn't mean you should throw yourself down a flight of stairs to try and duplicate Dorothy Eady's experience. Nor should you try to hypnotize your friends to see if one of them was Cleopatra or Elvis in a previous life. Hypnotic regression, like falling down stairs, is best left to the professionals. It should be done only by a trained therapist who can control the situation and head off problems.

There's a simpler and safer way of exploring the possibility of past lives. All you need is a notebook, a pencil, and an open mind.

Keeping a Past-Life Journal

Ever notice how sometimes you feel drawn to a certain part of the world, or to a particular period in history, for no logical reason? Or maybe you like a certain kind of food that nobody else in your family likes. Have you ever shown a natural talent for something, even though no one has taught you or even encouraged you to do it?

Some people believe that these kinds of unaccountable preferences and abilities are clues that can help us deduce what our past lives were like. They're the sorts of things you should record in your past-life journal.

Author Michael Talbot has a term for that inexplicable attraction you feel toward a particular time or place or activity; he calls it resonance. It's not the same as finding those things "interesting." It's more of a gut feeling, a nudge given to you by your unconscious mind.

After you've experienced resonance a few times, you'll probably learn to recognize the feeling. But in case you don't, here's a physical method of measuring resonance that may work for you.

Sit in a comfortable armchair with your forearms and hands lying on the arms of the chair; relax. Mentally ask your fingers to respond to your questions by wiggling a little. Now ask a question to which you know the answer is yes, and notice which finger wiggles.

Next, ask a definite "no" question; a different finger should move. Now you're ready to play a mystical version of Twenty Questions: "Did I live in America in a past life? In Europe? On this planet? Was I rich and famous? Was I such a loser that I don't really want to hear about it?" If neither your "yes" finger nor your "no" finger responds, or if a different finger moves, try rephrasing the question.

How do you go about finding the things that have resonance for you? A world atlas is a good place to start. Leaf through it, looking at the names of countries. If one really grabs you, write it down in your journal. Do the same with the names of cities or states or provinces within that country.

A historical museum is another good place to search for past-life clues. Take your journal along, and make a note of what time periods and what artifacts really speak to you. Have you always wanted one of those neat suits of armor, or a Native American head-dress, or a medieval tapestry? Can you picture yourself making adobe bricks, or manning a Civil War cannon, or panning for Klondike gold?

Check out an art museum, too, or even just an art book that covers various periods and styles. Do you feel you could step into a George Caleb Bingham painting of the frontier and feel at home? Or would you rather be sitting in one of Toulouse-Lautrec's French cafés?

Here are some other possible sources of clues to add to your journal.

"It is no more surprising to be born twice," wrote French author Voltaire, "than it is to be born once."

- The kinds of books you read. Do you tend to read a lot about one culture or area or time period?
- The pictures you put up on the walls of your room.
- The kind of house you'd most like to live in.
- Your hobbies. Do you collect coins? Stamps? Arrowheads?
- Your talents. Do you play a musical instrument? Are you an artist? Are you good with animals, or with machines?
- Your best subjects in school. Are you a math whiz? Do you pick up foreign languages easily? Any particular one? When you've done reports, what part of the world or period of history did you choose? Have you ever built a model of anything—the Globe Theatre, say, or a cliff dwelling?
- Your favorite foods. Do you like to eat Chinese or Mexican or Italian? Do you have a taste for spicy stuff, or tropical fruit?
- How climate and landscape affect you. Do you love hot summer days and hate the dead of winter, or the other way around? Do you yearn for some surroundings other than the ones you live in? The mountains? The ocean? The desert?
- Personality traits. Are you a leader or a follower? A big spender or a miser? Do you have any unreasonable fears?
- Names. Have you always liked a particular name? Have you ever felt that your own name doesn't suit you? What name does?
- Your younger years. When you were little, what games did you play? Did you prefer tea parties, or Cowboys and Indians? What toys were you crazy about? Soldiers? Fashion dolls? Horses, cars, or boats? Did you have an imaginary friend? What was that friend's name? Ask your parents if you came up with any odd words as a baby; write

them down and try to find out if they might be part of another language. Ask them if you ever talked about "when I used to be big."

• Dreams. These are an especially valuable source of information about past lives. Do you have one dream that keeps coming back? A particularly real-seeming dream? Do you ever dream of being in another time or place, or of wearing different clothing? After you've gathered a lot of clues about your past life or lives, and opened the door to your unconscious mind a little wider, you may find your dreams becoming more detailed and vivid. Be sure to record them in your notebook, too.

As you enter these items in your journal, be careful not to jump to conclusions. If you have a fascination with the life of Anne Frank, don't assume you were a European Jew or a Nazi soldier. Just because you like reading about the Battle of the Little Bighorn, that doesn't mean you were Custer or Crazy Horse. No single bit of information by itself is very significant. They're all just pieces of a puzzle. Only when they're fitted together do they give you the big picture.

Instant Karma

Even if you actually have lived before, what's the point in knowing about it? After all, it's over and done with. It's water under the bridge or over the dam, isn't it? Not according to most reincarnationists. They say that those past lives profoundly affect the one we're living now and that, furthermore, the life we live now can affect our future lives.

When Dr. Brian Weiss regressed a patient he calls Catherine, a voice spoke through her, and gave some insight into how one life is inextricably linked to the next: "We have debts that must be paid. If we have not paid out these debts, then we must take them into another life. . . . With each life that you go through and you did not fulfill these debts, the next one will be harder. If you fulfill them, you will be given an easy life. So you choose what life you will have."

Obviously that's just another way of stating the same thing that the law of karma says: "You reap what you sow."

Some reincarnationists suggest that, as the pace of modern life has increased, so has the pace of the reincarnation process. They say that many of us will manage to live through several different spiritual

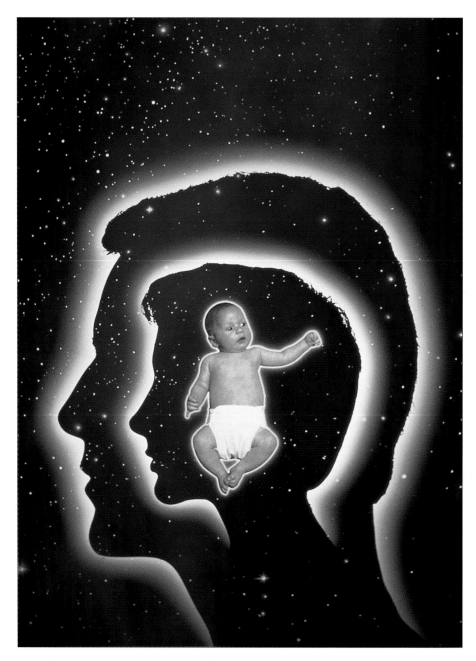

According to reincarnationists, our behavior in this life affects the kind of person we will be when we are born again.

lives in the course of one physical life, like a high school student who's also taking some first-year college courses. And the process of karma has geared up accordingly. Instead of reaping the results of what you sow in the next life, this theory says that it can happen in this life—"instant karma," they call it.

Whether or not this is true, it's not a bad idea to live your life as if it were true. Try hard to avoid the sorts of behavior that create bad karma—lying, cheating, rudeness, prejudice, greed, selfishness—and see what happens. Even if you don't come back for another turn on the wheel of life, you'll have made this life a lot more pleasant, and not just for yourself but for everyone around you.

That's the kind of life that's worth living all over again.

Glossary

age regression: A type of therapy in which the patient is hypnotized, then instructed to relive some earlier part of his or her life, in order to get at the root of a psychological problem.

automatic writing: Handwriting produced without conscious effort, while the writer is in a relaxed state or trance. Some believe the source of automatic writing is the subject's own unconscious mind; others say the words that are written are dictated by spirits of the dead.

Booth, John Wilkes (1838–1865?): A popular Shakespearean actor who supported the South during the Civil War. On April 14, 1865, Booth fatally shot President Lincoln. Most historians say Booth was killed by Union troops. Some, however, claim that his body was never positively identified.

Buddha: In Asian religion, an enlightened teacher. The most influential Buddha was Siddhārtha Gautama (about 563–483 B.C.), an Indian prince who founded the religion of Buddhism.

Caesar, Julius (100–44 B.C.): Roman general and historian who became dictator of Rome in 46 B.C.

Caldwell, Taylor (1900–1985): A popular American novelist, author of *Dear and Glorious Physician* and *The Captains and the Kings*.

Cayce, Edgar (1877–1945): An American psychic, called "the sleeping prophet." While in a trance, Cayce diagnosed illnesses and prescribed cures. Often, he blamed his patients' ailments on bad karma (see *karma*) carried over from a previous life.

déjà vu: The feeling of having already experienced events that are happening for the first time.

Eliot, George: The pen name of English novelist Mary Ann Evans (1819–1880), author of *Middlemarch* and *Silas Marner*.

Ford, Henry (1863–1947): American automotive pioneer. His use of the assembly line made the production of cars such as his Model T Ford quicker and cheaper.

Frank, Anne (1929–1945): A Jewish girl from Germany whose diary, written while she and her family hid from German soldiers in the Netherlands during World War II, was later published and widely read.

Gallup poll: A survey of public opinion on some issue, using market research methods developed by statistician George H. Gallup.

Gandhi, Mohandas (1869–1948): Indian political and spiritual leader whose nonviolent protests against British rule helped India gain its independence.

hieroglyphics: An early form of writing, using pictorial symbols.

karma: A concept held mainly by Buddhists and Hindus that says our behavior in this life determines what our next life will be like.

Kuala Lumpur: The capital city of Malaysia, a country in Southeast Asia.

Lebanon: A small country on the eastern shore of the Mediterranean Sea, bordered by Syria and Israel.

Mozart, Wolfgang Amadeus (1756–1791): One of the world's great composers, he began composing music at the age of five; at eight, he wrote his first symphony.

Ouija board: A board printed with numbers and letters. Players rest their fingers on a heart-shaped device that, in response to unconscious muscular movements—or, some say, the guidance of spirits—slides across the board to spell out a message.

pacifist: A person who believes in settling problems and differences without resorting to violence. Among famous pacifists were Mohandas Gandhi, Martin Luther King Jr., and Russian novelist Leo Tolstoy.

Pythagoras (about 580–500 B.C.): Greek philosopher and mathematician, best known for the Pythagorean theorem, quoted (incorrectly) by the Scarecrow in the movie *The Wizard of Oz*, after he gets his brain.

Twain, Mark: Pen name of Samuel L. Clemens (1835–1910), author of *The Adventures of Tom Sawyer* and *The Adventures of Huckleberry Finn*.

To Learn More about Past Lives

BOOKS-NONFICTION

Arvey, Michael. *Reincarnation: Opposing Viewpoints*. San Diego, CA: Greenhaven, 1989. Arguments both for and against the theory of reincarnation.

Atkinson, Linda. *Have We Lived Before?* New York: Dodd, Mead, 1981. Short, dramatized case histories of people who recalled past lives.

Green, Carl R., and William R. Sanford. *Recalling Past Lives*. Springfield, NJ: Enslow, 1993.

Moran, Michael, and Rachel Willen. *The Karma Violation Pad*. New York: Warner, 1991. A pad on which self-appointed "karma police" can write "tickets" for karma violations such as lying, cheating, and obnoxious behavior.

Schouweiler, Tom. *Life After Death*. San Diego, CA: Greenhaven, 1990. Thorough, balanced coverage of near-death experiences, various concepts of life after death, Ian Stevenson's studies. Lots of illustrations.

BOOKS-FICTION

Cavanagh, Helen. *The Last Piper*. New York: Simon and Schuster, 1996. Christie's five-year-old brother tells her convincing details about "when I was bigger."

Kehret, Peg. *Sisters, Long Ago*. New York: Cobblehill, 1990. Willow has visions of a former life as a twelve-year-old girl in ancient Egypt.

Kipling, Rudyard. "The Finest Story in the World." A short story about spontaneous memories of a past life; appears in many anthologies of Kipling's work.

ON-LINE INFORMATION *

http://www.cs.loyola.edu/~skgupta/#rein
   Spiritual Shack web page. Explanation of reincarnation and karma; information on how to get in touch with past lives.

http://www.inetport.com~one/bcrkpl.html
   Essay on reincarnation, karma, and past lives; question-and-answer session with the author of the essay.

http://www.spiritweb.org/Spirit/reincarnation.html
   Spirit Web website. Collection of articles on reincarnation, examples of past lives, information on past-life therapy, bibliography.

*Websites change from time to time. For additional on-line information, check with the media specialist at your local library.

Index

Page numbers for illustrations are in boldface.

INDEX

Notes

Quotations used in this book are from the following sources:

Page 10 "possibly the oldest": *Coming Back: A Psychiatrist Explores Past-Life Journeys* by Raymond A. Moody Jr., M.D. (New York: Bantam, 1990), p. 105.

Page 11 "As a man leaves": *Reincarnation: A Critical Examination* by Paul Edwards (Amherst, NY: Prometheus, 1996), p. 15.

Page 12 "I believe I shall": *Americans Who Have Been Reincarnated* by H. N. Banerjee, Ph.D., Sc.D. (New York: Macmillan, 1980), p. 5.

Page 12 "I think immortality": *Reincarnation: The Phoenix Fire Mystery* edited by Joseph Head and S. L. Cranston (New York: Julian Press, 1977), p. 338.

Page 12 "souls come and go": *Ford: The Men and the Machine* by Robert Lacey (Boston: Little, Brown, 1986), p. 234.

Page 13 "Work is futile": *Ford: The Men and the Machine*, p. 58.

Page 13 "The unit of life": *Reincarnation in World Thought* edited by Joseph Head and S. L. Cranston (New York: Julian Press, 1967), p. 398.

Page 19 "See, you chose me" and "Then I must": "Interview: Dr. Brian Weiss," *Omni* (April 1994), p. 88.

Page 21 "Even before I was recognized": *The Dalai Lama: A Policy of Kindness* edited by Sidney Piburn (Ithaca, NY: Snow Lion, 1990), p. 36.

Page 25 "It is nature's": *Reincarnation in World Thought*, p. 411.

Page 32 "I shudder": *The Search for a Soul: Taylor Caldwell's Psychic Lives* by Jess Stearn (Garden City, NY: Doubleday, 1973), p. 2.

Page 38 "I don't believe" and "they have crossed": *Your Past Lives: A Reincarnation Handbook* by Michael Talbot (New York: Fawcett Crest, 1987), p. 10.

Page 43 "some other place": *The Search for Bridey Murphy (New Edition)* by Morey Bernstein (Garden City, NY: Doubleday, 1965), p. 10.

Page 46 "Bridey was dead right": *The Search for Bridey Murphy*, p. 268.

Page 48 "God, I'm coming home": *The Reincarnation of John Wilkes Booth: A Study in Hypnotic Regression* by Dell Leonardi (Old Greenwich, CT: Devin-Adair, 1975), p. 171.

Page 50 "the subject's current personality": *Reincarnation in World Thought*, p. 434.

Page 51 "because they do not": *Reincarnation: A New Horizon in Science, Religion, and Society* by Sylvia Cranston and Carey Williams (New York: Julian Press, 1984), p. 54.

Page 52 "The case usually starts": *Here and Hereafter* by Ruth Montgomery (New York: Coward-McCann, 1968), p. 178.

Page 58 "knew the pictures": "The Dream Mother" by Cynthia Sanz and Ellin Stein, *People* (October 3, 1994), p. 80.

Page 58 "I want to go home" and "Here is my home": *Reincarnation: A New Horizon in Science, Religion, and Society*, p. 80.

Page 64 "It is no more surprising": *Reincarnation: A Critical Examination*, p. 20.

Page 67 "We have debts": *Many Lives, Many Masters* by Brian L. Weiss, M. D. (New York: Simon and Schuster, 1988), p. 172.

About the Author

Gary L. Blackwood is a novelist and playwright who specializes in historical topics. His interest in the Unexplained goes back to his childhood, when he heard his father tell a story about meeting a ghost on a lonely country road.

Though he has yet to see a single UFO or ghost, a glimpse of the future or a past life, the author is keeping his eyes and his mind open. Gary lives in Missouri with his wife and two children.